READ Our Book...

BEFORE You Buy or Adopt
a Dog...

BEFORE You Give Up On or
Get Rid of Your Dog...

BECAUSE You Love Your Dog...
Very Much!

Mark and Dru

Table of Contents

"An ounce of prevention is worth a pound of cure."

INTRODUCTION

The **number one reason** that well meaning, loving and caring, but frustrated owners **give up** their dogs to animal shelters is because of **behavior problems.** [1]

One of the **main causes of death** in puppies less than one year of age is said to be **euthanasia** due to **behavior problems.** [2]

Many owners are **unaware** of **all** the **important veterinary** care necessary and available for keeping their dog happy and healthy.

Because of this, they may not react quickly to changes in their dog's **health,** causing undo suffering and expense.

Unfortunately, when **training techniques** are **improperly** or **inadequately applied,** many dogs do not become trained to their owner's complete satisfaction and may even develop inappropriate behaviors secondary to the improper application of training techniques.

Each of these factors can threaten the potential for a satisfying and long-lasting relationship between dogs and their owners.

With a deepening **concern** for these issues, we were motivated to write this book in the hope that we could help you prevent training, medical and behavior problems from developing in your puppy or dog.

The overwhelming conclusion we have drawn as a result of the experiences we have had with thousands of dogs and their owners is that it is much **easier, prudent** and **humane to prevent dog problems** from developing than to try and change existing, established behaviors.

Our philosophy and methods have **proven** successful in **preventing** as well as **controlling,** tempering and in many cases alleviating **existing behavior problems**.

Our medical insight will help you to **maintain** your dog's good **health** and understand how medical changes may affect him and you.

Our training technique will **enhance** and **improve** your dog's response to **obedience training** commands.

In developing our philosophy and methods, we have drawn directly from the **needs** and **frustrations** of thousands of our clients.

We based this program on our appreciation of dogs as sentient creatures, realizing that they respond "**Best**" when treated with safe controls, management, respect, understanding, kindness, consistency, and of course, love.

Our philosophy and methods are endorsed by **veterinarians, humane societies, breeders** and other **professional dog trainers**.

These methods are **practical, easy** to understand and implement and have been developed for use in everyday life.

When used correctly, our methods are **safe** and **effective** and will not exacerbate existing conditions or create additional problems.

Our methods can be used for **all types** and sizes of dogs, from toys to giants, Yorkies to Mastiffs and everything in between.

Our program can be started on puppies as early as **eight weeks of age** or initiated with dogs at **any age**.

Being a **good** dog **owner** requires that you know your strengths and limitations as an effective care giver and dog trainer. Be smart and loving and know when to seek and accept help.

Have a strong "support team" available that includes a **veterinarian** and a **professional** dog **trainer.**

We encourage you to employ a professional dog trainer or enroll in a training course for the purpose of teaching your dog obedience. This will allow you to observe and experience the actual **physical** application of training techniques.

Successful obedience training will provide a line of communication between you and your dog, a language that you both can understand. This will enhance the development of a secure and happy relationship.

The close relationships we have developed with our own pet "family" has helped us immensely to understand the needs and wants of dogs and how to "Best Serve" them. We have learned much from them and they continue to teach us.

Above all else, they keep us **smiling.**

1. Miller DD, Staats SR, Partlo C, Rada K. Factors associated with the decision to surrender a pet to an animal shelter. JAVMA vol. 209, no. 4, (1996) 738-742.

2. Heath S: Puppies in your practice. Veterinary Practice Nurse 4(3): (1992) 29-30.

Use of "him," "his," "he" in this text refers to both male and female dogs and puppies.

———————————————

CHAPTER 1

TRAINING

EQUIPMENT

The training equipment you need will **depend** on the age, size, breed, temperament and coat texture of your puppy or dog. Equally important in the selection of equipment is the type of training you are involved in.

All dogs are **individuals**, so use the most humane equipment best suited to you, your dog and your situation.

If you are unsure of what to use or how to use it, ask a **professional** for advice. This will **prevent** undue **stress** and help alleviate possible **negative** repercussions that may result from using the wrong equipment.

The following equipment is what we find necessary for training all puppies and dogs.

Collars

1. A nylon or leather **buckle collar** is used for identification, initial obedience training and control. It should fit comfortably but snugly around his neck so that it will not slip off or pull over his head. When fitting it, you should be able to slide your finger between the collar and your dog's neck. You probably will have to adjust the collar or buy a larger size as your puppy grows.

2. There are other **specialized collars** available. The need for these will depend on how well your dog is responding to you and his training. These include:

Slip or "choke" collar made of nylon, leather or metal.

"Headcollar" which is a relatively new type of collar that fits comfortably over the dog's head. We have found it to be safe and effective for controlling and training puppies and dogs.

The use of any specialized training collars should be discussed with and **demonstrated** by an experienced dog trainer, veterinarian or pet shop professional **skilled** in the proper use of the particular collar.

6-ft training leash

We prefer leather or cotton leashes. We find them easier to grip and gentler on the hands than nylon or chain leashes.

This **leash** will be used as a "**communication tool**" for the purpose of managing your dog's unwanted behavior and teaching **proper**, socially acceptable responses. The six foot leash also enables you to teach and enforce obedience commands. (See pp. 11-14)

30-ft cotton training leash

The use of a 30-ft. leash will allow your dog to exercise, run and play outside while under your control (you must always hold the end of the leash.) It will prevent him from running away or getting lost and injured.

Because a dog responds to commands at a distance of 6 feet does not mean that he will obey and behave at a greater distance. Working with your dog on a 30-ft. leash is a prelude to teaching him advanced "Off-leash" obedience commands.

A 30-ft. training leash affords you the opportunity to teach and enforce obedience commands at long distances and enables you to instruct your dog to respond correctly in fun activities such as "Fetch."

You will have the additional benefit of effectively **controlling** and **correcting** from a distance, unwanted behaviors such as digging, excessive barking, chewing or eating unacceptable or harmful objects in the yard.

We recommend a 30-ft leash be used **carefully** by **adults** only.

Take care when you use it around other people to avoid any injuries that may occur as a result of you, others and your dog becoming entangled.

It is **not** to be used for tying the dog up.

CRATES
Keeping your dog safe

Our training method for controlling untrained puppies or dogs has evolved over the years from confining the dog in a small bathroom, kitchen or laundry room, to the **safer** and more **practical** use of a crate.

Crates are not cruel. In fact, they are a **safe** haven, comparable to a crib or playpen for an infant or toddler. When crates are **used properly**, most dogs will find security and comfort in the fact that the crate is their place or "den."

The **purpose** of a crate is to **prevent** the dog from getting in harm's way. It will also prevent any physical **destruction** to your home and possessions by the dog during the times when you cannot be with him. In addition, since dogs will try not to soil their sleeping area the utilization of a crate will help with the **housebreaking** process.

Buy a crate that will accommodate and be **comfortable** for your dog as he grows to physical maturity. He should be able to stand up, turn around, lie down and stretch out comfortably in it.

Line the crate with old or inexpensive towels. They are comfortable, absorbent and can be washed and reused. Keep them trimmed to prevent ingestion of loose threads.

Until your puppy is fully housebroken and beyond the point of destructive chewing, the initial use of these towels can be more practical than dog beds in the crate.

Many breeders use newspapers to line their kennel areas. Puppies may have become accustomed to urinating and defecating on them. If used to line their crate, the puppy may still associate the newspaper with this purpose.

Where *to place the crate*

Place the crate in an area that is frequented by the family, such as the kitchen or family room. Dogs are social animals and doing this will help him feel like he is part of the "clan."

When *to use the crate*

When you are out of the house, sleeping, cooking dinner or occupied with other daily activities that prevent you from being physically attached to your puppy or untrained dog on his leash, use the crate. The crate will keep him safe and out of harm's way, as well as protect your personal property.

Don't reserve the use of the crate exclusively for times when you are away from the home. The dog may begin to associate being put in the crate with you leaving the house.

Get him accustomed to being by himself in the crate when **you are home** as well. The dog will learn that it is okay for him to be by himself and you will help **prevent** separation anxiety from developing. (See p. 48)

Never use a crate for punishment. The crate should not be represented as a negative experience.

How *to use the crate*

1. Before placing your dog or puppy in the crate, make sure he has had a chance to **relieve** himself and has been **well exercised**.

2. When putting him in the crate use a consistent phrase such as "Kennel up!" given in an encouraging tone of voice. Initially, you can entice him in with a piece of dog food, small treat or one of his toys.

Leaving a bowl of food or water in the crate can **interfere** with housebreaking. If you are concerned about the amount of time in which you must leave your healthy puppy or dog confined to a crate without food or water, please consult your veterinarian.

3. Once he is in his crate, **remove** any **collars and leashes** for his safety. Close and secure the door.

From this point on, **do not speak to him** again while he is in the crate! This is very important! Talking to your dog can get him **excited** and may **heighten** any **anxiety** that he may have at the thought of being left alone. This can fuel the development of separation anxiety.

If he barks or whines, **do not** say or do anything! If you respond to the barking, you are teaching him that barking will get your attention.

If **all** his **needs** have been met (exercised, fed, watered and had an opportunity to relieve himself) he will eventually settle down.

4. When you approach the crate to take your pup out, **do not** speak to him. Talking to your dog or puppy at this time can overexcite him. This elevated state of exuberance can make him more difficult to control. Open the crate door and put the leash and collar on the dog while he is still in the crate. Lead him outside in a controlled manner. Allow him time to relieve himself and then tell him what a **"great"** dog he has been!

"...Dogs are not preprogramed with a computer chip on how to behave. They need to be taught!..."

PREVENT OBEDIENCE TRAINING PROBLEMS

To **prevent obedience training problems**, the most important fact to remember is that you must **always** be in the position to **enforce** your obedience commands. This is true for all training, all the time, and is **vital** to your success.

Your puppy or **untrained** dog should be kept on a 6-ft. training **leash** attached to you and in your **control** at **all** times when he is with you.

This enables you to always be in the position to **immediately, safely** and **effectively** teach, practice and enforce your obedience commands.

If the leash is not **held in your hand,** you are not able to give a quick, proper correction and you may have to chase after your dog in order to grab hold of the leash. This can teach him to run away from you and ignore your commands.

During the times when you cannot be present to physically control your untrained dog or puppy, he should be confined either inside, in a **"safe"** place such as a crate or outside in a **"safe"** and securely fenced area with adequate shelter from the elements.

Never give a training command to your untrained dog or puppy unless you are immediately able to safely and properly enforce it!

Your commands quickly lose their meaning when you are constantly repeating them and you are not in the position to **immediately** correct the dog for not responding properly.

"NO COMMANDS UNLESS YOU CAN ENFORCE THEM!"

If your dog has been **properly** taught and thoroughly understands obedience commands, it is appropriate for you to correct him when he does not respond to a command.

A **proper correction** is for the purpose of getting your dog's **attention**.

If he is not responding quickly to your first command, **immediately** give the leash a **quick snap** to get his attention and repeat the command. This instantaneous leash correction is the key to teaching your dog to respond quickly and consistently.

Repeat the process until the dog responds correctly. Then, vocally **praise, praise** and **praise** him.

A **lavish** amount of praise will encourage your dog to want to **give** and **repeat** the **correct** response.

This leash control must be maintained when you are with your dog, **inside** as well as **outside,** and should continue for a period of at least **six months to one year.** It takes **thousands of** successful responses to obedience commands over this amount of time for dogs to become consistent and reliable.

Many owners **mistakenly** believe that because their dog responds some of the time to a command, he knows to respond to the command all the time.

The truth is, dogs that have **not** been **taught correctly** respond when they feel like it, when they are bribed with food, or when they are physically intimidated to do so.

To be effective, the implementation of training techniques requires experience in the **proper application** of commands as well as the correct timing of praise and corrections.

We **strongly recommend** that you and your dog enroll in formal obedience training sessions. Successful training is best accomplished under the direction and in the physical presence of a professional trainer, be it private or in a group setting.

Your veterinarian is a good source for recommendations on classes and trainers in your area.

Dogs must be taught to respond consistently, under any distraction and in all circumstances. By keeping your puppy with you on his leash, you will be able to control him throughout the day and **incorporate** your **training** commands into your **everyday life,** which is the ultimate goal of every dog owner.

Off-leash Training

At the point in you and your dog's obedience training when he is responding to your commands in a consistent manner and under any and all circumstances, you can proceed to the next course known as **Advanced, "Off leash"** training.

This is an **extensive** and a much more challenging type of training. It should only be taught and practiced in the house or in a **controlled**, securely fenced outside area and preferably under the direction of a qualified, professional dog trainer.

Your puppy or dog may respond well in these controlled sessions. However, it takes, an absolute **minimum** of **six months** to **one year** for the advanced **training** to become **effective** and for the dog's "off leash" responses to be **reliable** in your environment.

We must **strongly caution** you to be prudent and extremely careful where and when you allow your dog "off leash." Even the best trained dogs may not respond 100% of the time in every situation.

Additional facts necessary to prevent obedience training problems

1. Begin training immediately. It is a scientific fact that puppies are capable of learning at eight weeks of age. Puppies tend to be more impressionable and physically easier to manage at this young age.

If you have an older puppy or untrained dog start training immediately as he can also learn and change.

2. Exercise your dog and allow him a chance to urinate and defecate before beginning your training session.

We suggest a minimum five minute exercise period. This tends to put the dog in a more relaxed frame of mind and allows him to focus on the training session.

3. Vocal praise is the best reward! It is always readily available. Dogs, like people, love a **generous** compliment of kind words! Food rewards are not always available and can be distracting.

4. The **tone of your voice** is important when giving a command to your dog. Remember that this is a **command** and not a request! Command the dog in a **firm** voice but do not yell or escalate the tone of your voice. Be consistent.

A quick and sharp **negative** tone should be used when **correcting** your dog but again, stay calm and do not yell.

A very **"happy, happy"** tone of voice should be used to express your pleasure when **praising** your dog.

5. Stay calm. Do not yell, get angry or frustrated. If you do, you may cause the dog to become overexcited or he may "freeze" and shut you out.

Limit the force of your physical leash corrections. If your dog does not respond to your first command, give his leash a quick snap (solely for the purpose of getting his attention) and repeat the command. This technique should **only** be **applied** and will **only** be **effective** with dogs that have been **properly taught** obedience commands.

When dogs are properly trained with consistency, persistence, patience, understanding and an abundance of **praise, praise** and more **praise**, the chance of a **positive response** is greatly enhanced.

6. All family members should be involved in the obedience training of the dog or puppy so that he learns to respond appropriately to each member of the family.

Initially, the training is best performed by adult family members. When the adults have established good control and command over the dog or puppy, the younger members of the family should become involved in the training under adult supervision. Continuity and consistency will make it easier for the dog to respond appropriately.

CHAPTER 2

MEDICAL

PREVENT MEDICAL PROBLEMS

As with people the key to your dog's good health is a **comprehensive, preventive** medical program.

Preventing medical problems from developing is beneficial to your dog's **well being**, is **cost**

effective, and will eliminate the potential anxiety and stress associated with illness. Your dog's longevity and good health can be directly related to the time and effort you put into maintaining his health.

Develop a relationship with your veterinarian. Allow him or her to aid and guide you through the necessary steps and procedures for securing a healthy life for your pet.

Your dog or puppy should undergo a comprehensive **health examination** by your veterinarian within the **first few days** after you bring him home. At this first checkup you can discuss proper diet and a follow up preventive health care plan for your pup.

Health problems particular to your puppy's breed can be discussed or detected.

Some breeds are prone to developing certain medical problems (hip dysplasia, heart problems, eye diseases, skin conditions.) Your veterinarian can discuss these with you.

Certain breeds may require more attention to areas such as routine grooming and eye and ear care. Your veterinarian can point out potential problem areas and show you ways to **prevent problems** from developing.

Your veterinarian will recommend an appropriate examination schedule based on the individual needs, age and health status of your dog.

Puppies require an initial exam and series of vaccinations.

Adult dogs should be examined at least annually for preventive health care and to receive any necessary **booster** vaccinations.

"Senior" dogs at around seven years of age can begin to have additional medical and nutritional needs and may experience behavioral changes. Your veterinarian may suggest blood tests to keep on top of your dog's aging system.

VACCINATIONS

There are a number of diseases for which **all** dogs and puppies should be vaccinated. This may vary depending upon what part of the country you live in and the exposure risks for your dog.

Please **consult your veterinarian** for his or her recommendations as to what initial **vaccines** or **boosters** are necessary for your dog.

The following is a list of vaccines that you should be aware of:

1. DHLP- Distemper, hepatitis, parainfluenza, leptospirosis

2. Parvo virus
3. Corona virus
4. Rabies
5. Bordetella ("Kennel Cough")
6. Lyme disease

In addition to vaccinations, your dog should also be routinely examined (at least yearly) for internal and external **parasites** such as:

1. Heart worm -This deadly parasite is transmitted by mosquitoes and detected by a blood sample. Depending upon where you live or travel with your dog, he may require medication to prevent heartworm disease.
2. Intestinal parasites -Detected in a fecal sample and include hookworms, roundworms, coccidia, tapeworms.
3. Fleas, Ticks and Mites

Great advances have been made in the area of parasite control. Ask your veterinarian what is necessary and best to use for your puppy or dog.

PROPER DIET AND NUTRITION

Always feed a good quality dog food. The type can vary depending on the age, breed, activity level and medical condition of your dog. **Consult** with your veterinarian, trainer or a knowledgeable pet store professional for type and suggested feeding schedule.

Choose a quality dog food that suits you and your dog and stick with it. Changing brands and sometimes even the flavor of the food can cause gastrointestinal problems (vomiting and/or diarrhea) or create "picky" eating habits.

A good quality dog food will contain all the necessary ingredients to keep your dog healthy and satisfied. Normal, healthy dogs and puppies that are on a good quality, nutritional dog food do not require additional **dietary supplements**. Consult with your veterinarian before giving any to your dog, as some supplements can actually be harmful.

We prefer dry food over canned because it is better for the teeth (keeps them cleaner as more time is spent chewing) and is more convenient to use.

Always check with your veterinarian before feeding "**people food**" or table scraps to your dog. In addition to the possibility of causing **vomiting** or **diarrhea**, some foods can cause severe illnesses, such as a form of hemolytic anemia linked to the ingestion of onions by dogs.

Do not overfeed! **Obesity** is a **major health problem** with dogs in the United States. It is associated with the same health problems as it is in people. (Stress on cardiovascular system and skeletal system, i.e., joints, knees, hips.) Adjust the amount of food according to your dog's age, current weight and activity level allowing for growth and weight maintenance.

Feeding **"treats"** is fine when done in **moderation** and as long as it does not prevent the dog from eating a normal amount of dog food. Remember that treats have **calories** and can quickly add **excess pounds** to your "pooch."

As your **dog ages**, his **dietary needs** may change. His metabolism and activity level can slow down and his absorption of nutrients from the food may decrease. Tooth loss and gum disease may alter his ability to chew. Certain age related medical conditions may require special dietary considerations. Consult with your **veterinarian** for his or her specific recommendations on the **nutrition** of your **"senior"** dog.

Keeping your puppy on a **leash, attached** to you will help **control** what he puts in his mouth. **Ingestion** of foreign objects like rocks, sticks, articles of clothing, garbage, household poisons or toys can cause diarrhea, vomiting or intestinal obstructions and may even result in the death of your dog.

DENTAL CARE

Teach puppies early to allow you to open their mouths to examine and **clean** their **teeth**. Your veterinarian can demonstrate proper ways to do this. If you cannot do this regularly and effectively, it will be necessary to have your dog's teeth cleaned periodically by your veterinarian.

Dog foods specifically formulated to help **prevent** the formation of **tartar** are currently available. Consult your veterinarian or pet store professional.

Your dog's oral hygiene is just as important as your own. **Gingivitis** can lead to tooth decay and subsequent loss of teeth. The bacteria that enter the bloodstream through infected, irritated gums can find a way into the heart of your dog, eventually resulting in **heart disease.**

If at any time you notice any changes in the odor of your dog's breath or problems chewing or swallowing, you should consult your veterinarian.

It is important to get in the habit of **physically examining your dog every day.** It will only take you a few minutes and he will probably enjoy the attention!

The examination process can also aid in teaching your dog to **accept** and **tolerate** handling of his body parts. (see Preventing Inappropriate Aggression, pp. 53-54.)

Check his **ears** (inside and out) for redness, cuts, swellings or discharge. Check **eyes** for abnormal tearing, redness or discharge. Run your hands over his body and feet looking for fleas, ticks, cuts, bruises or lumps. Monitor his normal daily eating, drinking, urinating and defecating patterns.

Know what is normal for your dog. The **quicker** you **detect** a problem or deviation from the norm, the more effective you will be in dealing with the situation.

HORMONAL INFLUENCE ON BEHAVIOR

"Heat" cycles in an intact **female** dog can disrupt normal behavior. This is caused by the rise and fall of hormone levels.

Housebreaking accidents can occur. Appetite can decrease. In an attempt to "nest," female dogs may dig or scratch up carpeting or shred their bedding. Some may show aggression over their possessions or become secretive and hide things.

Intact **male** dogs can be more aggressive with other dogs and people including family members. They may tend to roam more. Marking behavior due to hormonal influence may affect housebreaking. Appetite can decrease if the dog is within "scent" of a female dog in heat.

We recommend **spaying** or **neutering** your puppy or dog. Contrary to what many owners believe, neutering and spaying does not change a dog's basic disposition or personality in any negative way. Neutered and spayed dogs have **fewer health problems** associated with the reproductive tract such as mammary cancer and testicular tumors. They also tend to **live longer.** Consult your veterinarian for his or her recommendation as to what age these surgeries should be performed.

EXERCISE

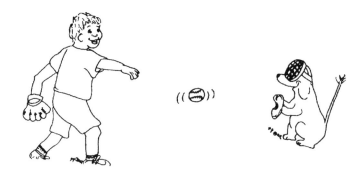

Exercise is **vital** to your dog for his mental and

physical well being. To **prevent** medical or behavioral problems, you must provide enough proper exercise for your dog. A **bored** dog, who turns his energy into a self mutilating activity, can develop a "lick granuloma" from constant, excessive chewing or licking of a leg or paw.

Obesity due to a lack of exercise affects the inactive, "couch potato" dog in much the same way as it does humans. Excessive weight can **decrease** your dog's normal life span.

You and your dog will **both benefit** from an interactive exercise and training program.

THE GERIATRIC DOG

Unfortunately, we cannot prevent our dogs from aging. We can, however, help to **maintain** the best **quality of life** possible for them by being aware of the effects that age related **medical** and **physiological changes** can have on our dogs' **behavior.**

The acuity of the senses of sight, smell and hearing are reduced with age making a dog less reactive to commands. **Excessive barking** can develop as he becomes confused or "lost" in his environment. **Tolerance** of stimuli, even touching and petting, can change.

Dogs may become **less responsive** to commands or even **aggressive** when osteoarthritis affects their mobility and causes pain on moving or being touched. **Decreased mobility** can also affect housebreaking, as the dog is hesitant or unable to move to its usual spot to relieve himself.

A previously well behaved and well trained older dog that **suddenly** begins to demonstrate **inappropriate behavior** should be evaluated by your veterinarian as a medical disease could be the root of the problem.

For example, urinary tract or kidney disease

can cause incontinence and therefore affect housebreaking. Hypothyroidism can result in decreased activity or responsiveness, irritability or even aggression.

Diagnosing underlying medical conditions and initiating treatment for them can help to alleviate or cure associated "behavioral" symptoms. Advances in canine geriatric nutrition and medications available to control pain from osteoarthritis can help you and your dog enjoy his "senior" years.

COGNITIVE DYSFUNCTION

With aging a dog's brain can undergo a series of changes that may result in a cognitive decline.
What used to be called "Old Dog Syndrome" or senility, is now referred to as "Cognitive Dysfunction."

Cognitive Dysfunction is an age-related deterioration of a dog's memory, perception and awareness of its surroundings characterized by behavioral changes **not** associated with a medical disease.
Affected dogs can act disoriented or confused, become trapped in corners, get lost

behind furniture, or stare into space. They may react differently to family members, interact less or even exhibit aggression. Housebreaking "accidents" occur. Sleeping patterns may change with the dog sleeping more during the day and being awake in the middle of the night.

There is a drug that has been approved for the treatment of "Cognitive Dysfunction" in dogs. It may help to alleviate some of the symptoms of this disorder in your dog.

Please talk to your veterinarian about any problems you may be experiencing with your "senior" dog.

CHAPTER 3

BEHAVIOR

PREVENT BEHAVIOR PROBLEMS

"Most dogs will not act out with inappropriate or obsessive behaviors when properly exercised, physically and mentally."

Mark Katz

Dogs have certain breed characteristics developed for the purpose of performing a

— TRACKING —

—HERDING—

particular job, be it herding . . .

retrieving, guarding or hunting. They come with all the **energy** necessary to perform this function all day long!

- SEARCH AND RESCUE -

To **prevent** behavior problems from developing and also to dramatically reduce or resolve existing behavior problems, this energy needs to be **channeled and controlled.**

- PEST CONTROL -

Though it isn't always possible for you to provide your

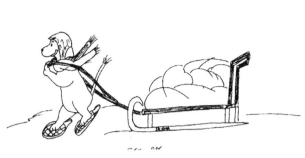

- SLED DOG -

dog with the working career for which he may have been intended, it is **always** possible to **provide alternative activities** as an outlet for his energy.

Obedience training sessions, teaching tricks, playing interactive games such as fetch . . .

and "hide and go seek" with your dog . . .

or physical exercise in the form of walks, running, or agility training courses . . .

can all provide good **physical and mental exercise** for your dog.

"By taking **immediate** action to correct inappropriate behavior you are preventing the development of serious problems. By **not** correcting inappropriate behavior, you are allowing it to exist and develop further."

The methods we employ for preventing problem behaviors can be used to **control, manage** and **alleviate** many behavior problems that have already taken root.

The most effective way to teach your puppy or dog "right from wrong" is to always be in the position to **immediately** correct inappropriate behavior and reinforce proper behavior.

Dogs learn **"Best"** and the effects are most **lasting** when corrections are given **during** the inappropriate act and praise is given **immediately** after an appropriate response.

This is accomplished by always maintaining control of your puppy or untrained dog on a 6-ft. training **leash** with you holding the other end. When he acts inappropriately quickly snap the leash in order to get his "attention" and at the same time say "No!" in a firm tone of voice. **Do not yell!**

When correcting your puppy, it is important not only to **stop** the inappropriate behavior but at the same time **redirect** him to an acceptable, **positive** alternative and acknowledge his good behavior with lots of **praise**. As an example, if your puppy or dog jumps up on you, snap the leash and say "No!" Command him to "Sit" and when he does tell him what a **great** dog he is.

The **consequence** of not keeping your untrained dog or puppy on a leash, with you **holding** the other end, is that you will not be in the position to give a **proper** and **immediate** correction and he will **not associate** the correction with his inappropriate behavior.

You may have to **chase** after your puppy in order to **grab** hold of his leash to correct him. This can teach him to **run away** from you.

In addition, if you have to reach down to grab the leash, your dog may respond defensively in anticipation of a correction, becoming **aggressive, nervous** or **shy**.

When you are not able to **hold** on to the 6-ft leash your puppy or untrained dog should be kept in a "**safe**" area such as a crate or securely fenced outside area. (Remember to **always** remove the leash and training collar when confining your dog to avoid any entanglement that can result in injury to your dog.)

"While it is important for you to be your dog's leader, the **emphasis** should be on **how** you achieve this."

Mark and Dru Katz

Let the "**Buyer beware!**" Training methods that advocate hitting, shaking or other means of physically threatening your puppy **cannot** be safely instituted by all members of the family. We **do not** recommend that anyone use these techniques.

In many cases, these methods will **create** or **exacerbate behavior problems** such as **aggression, shyness** or **submissive urination.**

Be **kind, understanding** and **fair** when correcting your puppy and **emphasize** the **praise** when an appropriate response is given.

It is essential to understand that your **success** will **correlate** directly with your formal **knowledge** of dog behavior.

Dogs use **body language** and vocalizations to **communicate** their feelings to other animals and humans.

A dog can display a **variety** of physical

postures at the **same time** in response to a particular stimulus. The dog may be experiencing conflicting feelings about the situation or stimulus. This can give the owner a confused message.

The **same posture** can signify a variety of **very different** feelings. A dog can wag his tail not only when he is happy, but also when he is excited, nervous, aggressive or even fearful. When a dog pins his ears back, it can indicate extreme aggression or it may be a simple expression of submissiveness.

It takes **formal knowledge** of dog behavior and an abundance of **"dog experience"** to be able to accurately **interpret** the conflicting signals that a dog can exhibit. A correct **analysis** is necessary to respond appropriately and **effectively** to a dog's behavior.

If your dog or puppy seems **"out of control"** and you are having difficulty communicating with him we encourage you to enlist the aid of a qualified dog trainer or behaviorist. These **professionals** can evaluate your situation and interpret your dog's physical manifestations, reactions and responses. They know **when** and **how** to correct and reward your dog and most important, they have the ability to teach **you** how to do this.

If your dog or puppy exhibits an **obsessive** behavior (tail chasing, excessive licking or chewing of his body parts), a **sudden** behavioral change or an **extreme** personality change ("friendly" to "aggressive"), we recommend an **immediate consultation with your veterinarian.** There may be a medical component that is the root of the behavior.

SOCIALIZATION

Socialization is the process of learning appropriate social behavior.

No, you don't need to take your dog out dancing, but you do need to **expose** him to all types of **social experiences**.

The **socialization** period is a **critical time** in the mental development of a puppy. It is during this time that social attachments to people are made.

During this important time in his life, the experiences your dog has will have long-lasting effects on how he will react in the future to adults, children, noises, dogs, cats, other animals and novel situations.

There exists a **very narrow time frame** for you to successfully **socialize** your puppy. The **ideal "socialization period"** begins around three weeks of age and continues to about 12 weeks of age.
Though successful socialization becomes increasingly more difficult to achieve as a puppy gets older, utilizing our program can help improve your older puppy or dog's social behavior and is well worth the effort.

Most puppies are kept with their mother and litter mates at the breeder's until 8 weeks of age. The process of **socialization** should **begin** with the **breeder** and **continue** with the new **owner**.

Before initiating contact with the "outside world" make sure your puppy is **healthy** and current with all necessary **immunizations**. To prevent illnesses, do not allow him to interact with dogs of unknown health or vaccination history or sniff other animal feces.
Control him on a leash for his safety.

To **develop** into a **friendly** and **confident** adult dog, puppies should be exposed to many new situations and environments, people and other animals.

The **process of socialization** should:

1. Not be delayed because of adverse, seasonal weather conditions. Waiting till the spring to socialize the "winter" puppy is not acceptable. Socialization **cannot** wait!

2. Include exposure and interaction with other adults and children besides those in your immediate family. Do this both at your home and other locations. Playgrounds, pet stores and strip shopping malls are great places to do this.

The **consequences** of not socializing your dog with people other than your immediate family can be a dog that is frightened of or fearfully aggressive toward unfamiliar adults or children.

3. Bring the puppy with you in the car as **often** as possible so that he will become accustomed to riding in the car and be comfortable when traveling.

~ TAKE HIM FOR CAR RIDES ~

Take the necessary safety precautions in the car. Put the puppy in a crate, use a specially designed harness that attaches to a seat belt, or let a responsible person control him.

4. Expose your puppy to various sights and sounds, bicycles, trains, trucks, traffic noises, and kids running and playing in a variety of locations.

The **consequences** of not exposing your puppy to a large variety of unfamiliar noises and surroundings, other than his immediate home environment can be **fear-based anxiety** and the desire to flee from any unfamiliar noise, place or situation.

5. Include socializing your puppy with other dogs. This is a great way for him to learn about **relationships**, not only with other **canines**, but with other **people** as well.

Make sure that:
1. All dogs involved are **healthy** and **current** with their vaccinations.
2. All dogs are initially **leashed** and held by their respective owners so that you can monitor and control their reactions to each another.
3. All dogs are **compatible** with one another. Interaction is best and safest with dogs of a

comparable temperament, age and size.

Some dogs, due to a genetic or breed disposition, may never look to play or interact with other dogs. **Don't force** the issue.

As dogs mature, their attitudes toward other **dogs** may **change,** regardless of their early positive interactions.

In all instances, however, **you** should be able to **control** your dog and make him **tolerate** the presence of other dogs.

The effort and time you take to properly socialize your puppy will be well worth the end result of a **confident, relaxed** and **well-adjusted** dog that is **welcomed** by all and a **joy** to live with!

SEPARATION ANXIETY

Dogs are highly social animals. In the wild, canines live in family groups. When dogs live with people, they become part of our family unit. Being left alone is unnatural and can result in distress or what is commonly known as "separation anxiety."

Most dogs experience some degree of anxiety when they are left alone. Their owners are usually unaware of this stress until the anxiety intensifies and begins to manifest itself in some form of undesirable or destructive behavior.

Separation anxiety is most commonly evidenced when a dog is left alone in the house for a long period of time. It can also occur when a dog is left alone in a room, a car or even outside in a yard.

Typical **manifestations of separation anxiety** are

1. Excessive barking or howling when left alone.

2. Inappropriate defecation or urination when left alone.

3. Destructive chewing or scratching of windows, walls, doors, digging up of carpet and flooring in front of closed doorways when left alone.

4. Self mutilation behavior which can result in the formation of lick granulomas.

5. Aggression exhibited toward the owners when they leave the house.

Once established, separation anxiety can be frustrating to treat. It is much **easier** to **prevent** the anxious behavior from ever becoming extreme.

To prevent separation anxiety

1. Leave your puppy or dog alone for short periods of time from the very beginning. We recommend using a crate for his safety (Consult pp. 7-9 on crate training.)

Leave him in the **crate** when you go **out** of the house. Put him in the crate when **you are in** the house as well. Leave him in it while you are in another room so that he won't associate being placed in the crate with your leaving the house.

Outside, leave him alone in a safe and secure area of the yard for short periods of time while you are in the house.

2. Avoid creating a **"fuss"** when leaving or coming home to your dog and when taking him in and out of his crate. **Don't talk** to him while he is in the crate. This can create anxiety.

As dog owners, many of us no doubt experience our own anxiety and guilt over leaving our dogs alone. This may encourage us to overindulge our dogs with attention when we leave them home alone or when we return home to them. This can add "fuel" to their anxiety.

3. Provide a **special** toy or treat given **only** when your puppy or dog is in his crate. This can help him associate the crate with a positive experience.

4. Do not **elevate** your dog or puppy to a point of human equality by feeding him from the table or allowing him in your bed or on the couch as this may **increase** the tendency for separation **anxiety** to develop.

5. Teach him **obedience** commands. Dogs that respond well to the discipline and structure of obedience training tend to be more **confident, secure** and **calm** in any situation.

6. **Exercise** and play with your dog before you leave him. This can help him to relax and be comfortable when left alone.

There can be a **genetic** influence on your dog's disposition that may play a role in the development of excessive separation anxiety.

If you feel that your pet has an overabundance of anxiety, shyness or fears, please consult immediately with your **veterinarian** and a competent professional **trainer** or **behaviorist** to evaluate and treat the problem.

Pharmaceutical treatment for separation anxiety is currently available. All drugs **must** be prescribed and monitored by your veterinarian.

Unfortunately, these drugs by themselves are rarely a cure.

Drug therapy should not be looked upon as a "quick fix," but rather as an adjunct treatment to be used initially in conjunction with a proven, professionally applied, **behavior modification** program.

AGGRESSION

Aggression is a natural, instinctive behavior necessary for a canine's **survival** in the **wild**.

Because our dogs live with us in a **civilized** society, they must be taught how to **control** this normal, survival quality.

We define **aggressive behavior** as any type of combative or threatening gestures by your dog toward you, another person or animal.

Included in this definition is baring teeth, barking in a threatening manner, growling, mouthing and biting.

Over the years, we have heard **owners** give every **excuse** there is for why their dog exhibited **inappropriate** aggression: . . . "I woke him up" . . . " I went near his food" . . . " I tried to take his toy away" . . . "He doesn't like me to touch his feet" . . .

Yes, we can, in most cases, define the intention and cause for a dog's aggressive act.

However, the only aggression we deem acceptable is in the form of barking for the purpose of **alerting** and **alarming** you to the presence of persons on your property, at your door, approaching your vehicle or in response to the potential threat of bodily harm to you or a family member. This normal, **protective behavior** is acceptable as long as you are **totally in control** of the dog and he is otherwise **safe** for people to be around.

The concern of many owners is the notion that by **correcting inappropriate** aggression they will inhibit their dog's protective qualities. This is not the case.

Preventing and **controlling inappropriate** aggression **will not** interfere with a dog's **natural tendency** to protect "his" home and family.

**Uncontrolled, inappropriate aggression is potentially dangerous to you and all involved with the dog.

We do not recommend that you attempt to resolve any established or intensifying aggression issues on your own, especially when children are involved. The aggression can escalate and you or someone else can be seriously injured in the process.

Aggression is a complex issue. The **treatment** of aggression problems requires the help of an **experienced professional**. (Veterinarian, behaviorist, trainer or combination of all three.)

The reason for the aggression must be

correctly identified.

Proper **medical therapy** may need to be utilized along with **behavioral** modification **techniques** for the best chance of achieving a positive result.

To Prevent Inappropriate Aggression

We recommend the following preventive measures be used **only** for puppies or dogs with **no previous** or **existing** inappropriate aggression. They should be performed **initially** by **adult** family members. If at any time your dog or puppy begins to exhibit **any** growling or aggressive behavior **immediately** seek **professional** help. The problem will only escalate if not treated promptly and correctly.

1. Always be in the position to properly **manage** your puppy's **behavior** with him on a 6-ft training **leash attached** to you.

2. After adult members of the family have had consistently positive responses from the dog or puppy other family members should become involved in his handling, feeding and training. (**Children always under adult supervision.**) This way, your dog will learn how to respond in a positive manner to and respect **all members** of the family.

3. Puppies and dogs need to develop a **tolerance** for being **touched** and **handled** for the purposes of grooming (nail cutting, cleaning ears and eyes, brushing and bathing) accepting medications, as well as for receiving affection.

Inspect and **touch** different parts of his **body**. Say the name of each body part as you touch it ("mouth", "foot", "ear", "tail".) Gently put your fingers in his mouth and say "Open" while you teach him to open his mouth.

Gently **roll him over** and say "Over" and gently rub his belly. This command will allow you to inspect his underside when necessary and has the extra added benefit of teaching him to "submit to your will."

4. Growling over food, toys or bedding stems from a survival instinct to protect what a dog deems to be "his." This may be a natural behavior for a dog in the wild but it is **totally unacceptable** in your family setting or environment.

Feed your puppy a few pieces of his dog **food** by hand before you put his bowl of food on the floor. While he is eating, gently pet him and place your hand in his food dish.

Once the dog has responded positively with the adults, the whole family (children under adult supervision) should take turns feeding the dog so that he will look to all members as a food source.

If you have a multiple pet household (other dogs, cats, rabbits, ferrets) keep them separated when they are being fed. A dog can become protective of "his" food and may exhibit aggression when another pet approaches his food dish.

Hold or take his **toy** away from him when he is playing with it. (**Use** the **"Drop It"** command: see Destructive Chewing, p. 61-62.) **Replace** the toy with another one or give back the one he allowed you to take from him. And **always,** when he responds correctly, **praise, praise, praise** him!

Sit down next to him and **pet him** while he is in his own dog **bed.**

Children can perform these exercises, but **only** under strict **adult supervision** and **only after** the dog has demonstrated consistently positive responses for the adults in the family, displaying **absolutely** no evidence of aggression.

5. We do not recommend the puppy or dog be allowed up on your bed or furniture.

When you elevate him to your level by allowing

this, in his mind he becomes your equal in the family unit. Because of this, he may become protective of what he perceives to be "his" furniture and show aggression when you or others approach him.

Our recommendation for "snuggling" with your dog is to do it on the floor on a rug, blanket or big "dog" bed.

6. Playing rough with your dog or puppy can **stimulate aggressive** behavior.

We do not recommend playing games such as **"tug of war"**or **wrestling** with your dog as this can encourage him to **"fight"** with you.

Do not allow children to overexcite him. Allowing your dog to chase you or your children can initiate a natural predatory stalking response in him, resulting in nipping or biting.

7. Correctly **socialize** your puppy (see Chapter 3: Socialization, pp. 42-46.)

8. Follow your veterinarian's recommendations for **spaying** or **neutering** your puppy to eliminate the **hormonal influence** on inappropriate aggression.

Aggression in Aging dogs

The infirmity associated with **aging**, developing medical conditions and hormonal imbalances can all have an **effect** on an older dog's mental state and his **tolerance** level for external stimuli, new situations and interactions with people. (refer to The Geriatric Dog pp. 30-32.)

As dogs age, aggressive behavior may develop in response to **physical pain** from conditions such as arthritis.

Decreased awareness of his surroundings due to failing vision, hearing or sense of smell can cause an old dog to take up a "defensive" posture and react aggressively when woken up, startled or touched.

If your older dog begins to exhibit any inappropriate aggression, **consult** with your veterinarian **immediately**.

PUPPY NIPPING

Dogs use their **mouths** in their interaction with others like we use **our hands.**

As we **teach** our children to use their hands in a proper and gentle manner, we need to **instruct** dogs to exercise sensitivity and control when using their mouths.

Puppies must be taught early on that nipping is unacceptable.

To correct your puppy when he is nipping you or someone else, snap the leash to get his **attention** and say, "No!" in a calm, firm voice. **Do not over react**! Yelling and getting angry with him can cause your puppy to nip more aggressively.
As soon as he responds to the leash correction and stops nipping, **praise** him and **give** him one of his toys to chew or play with, thereby redirecting his **need** to use his mouth.

Sometimes putting a bitter tasting, nontoxic substance on your hand, such as lemon juice, hot pepper or mustard can help to deter the nipping.

Another alternative that we find **effective** and that can be **satisfying** to the puppy is to

teach him to **lick** your hand. Whenever he licks your hand, say "Lick, Lick, Lick." You can rub something he likes the taste of on your hand (peanut butter) until he gets the idea! Then, whenever he nips or "mouths" your hand, give him a proper correction (see p. 58) and then give him the positive alternative command to "Lick, Lick."

And, of course, always remember to give him **lots of praise** when he does what you ask him to do!

If your puppy continues to nip consider the following:

1. He may need **more** interactive play and exercise to channel his energy.

2. He may be **overstimulated** or **overtired** and in need of a **nap**! **Calmly** put him in his crate.

3. You may need to focus **more** attention on his obedience training which will give you better control over his behavior.

If you are unsuccessful in your attempt to stop the nipping or have a question about your implementation of these techniques, **immediately consult** your **veterinarian** or a **professional dog trainer** before the problem escalates.

DESTRUCTIVE CHEWING

Chewing is a completely **normal and natural** behavior for puppies and dogs.

Dogs chew:
1. For **nourishment** - looking for food items to sustain their existence.
2. Out of **boredom** - it's something to do.
3. Due to **teething** - to dislodge deciduous, baby teeth.
4. From **stress** - as a result of uncontrolled separation anxiety.

When dogs chew **inappropriate** or unsafe objects, it can be **harmful** not only to your belongings, but to your dog as well.

To prevent destructive chewing

1. Management is the key!

To control your puppy or untrained dog when you are with him, keep him **attached** to you with a 6 ft. training leash to prevent his access to unsuitable and dangerous objects.

In the event that it becomes necessary to correct your dog you will be in the best position to **immediately** effect a **proper** correction which is the

most effective way to achieve successful, long-lasting results.

Whenever you cannot be physically attached to your puppy or untrained dog he should be kept in his crate or other "safe" area out of "harm's way."

2. When your dog attempts to chew an inappropriate object, quickly snap the leash to get his **attention** and in a firm voice say "No!" **Immediately** provide him with one of his toys and give him lots of **praise, praise** and **praise**.

He will learn what he **should not** chew and most important, what he **should** chew.

If a toy is not readily available, correct your puppy and then utilize an obedience command, such as "Sit", "Down", "Stay" or "Heel." When he responds correctly, always **praise, praise** and **praise** him.

If your dog already has an inappropriate object in his mouth, calmly pull up on his leash in a slow, steady manner. This should cause his jaw to slacken slightly. **Do not** pull the dog up off his feet. Calmly, say **"Drop it." Do not yell**. Remove the item from the dog's mouth, **praise** him lavishly for releasing it, and if readily available **replace** it with one of his chew toys.

An alternative to this is to draw his attention to one of his toys enticing him to play with it and thus drop the object he has in his mouth. When he responds correctly **praise, praise** and **praise** him.

"**Drop it**" is a very important and useful command to teach your dog as it is inevitable that he will pick up inappropriate or potentially harmful objects with his mouth. **Practice** this command often with his toys. Don't wait until you need it.

Dogs can be tenacious and unyielding when asked to give up what they perceive to be a "treasure." If you are having difficulty teaching your dog to release his "trophy" do not force the issue. Please **consult** a professional trainer for "hands on" visual instruction for teaching this command.

3. **Limit** the **types** of toys or chew objects to four or five. Limiting the types of toys makes it easier for your dog to **identify** "his stuff."
    We **do not** suggest using old socks, shoes, gloves or other personal items as toys since the dog may not discriminate between "his" shoes and yours. These items can also be harmful if swallowed in part or whole. Discuss with your veterinarian what types of toys are best for you and your dog.
    Keep one of **each type** of toy in each room your dog is allowed so that they are always readily available for him.

4. Boredom is a major reason why puppies and dogs get into "trouble."

We cannot stress enough the importance of **proper, interactive exercise** and **play** (see p. 35-36) in alleviating destructive chewing, as well as other problem behaviors.

5. Don't assume that once a puppy has all his adult teeth he will stop chewing. It can take up to **one year** and hundreds of repetitions for your dog to learn what is appropriate and acceptable for him to chew.

Adhere to these simple procedures and you can in most cases control and prevent destructive chewing.

If your dog seems to **excessively** seek **abnormal** items to chew or ingest, **consult** your **veterinarian**. Certain medical conditions or dietary deficiencies may be the cause.

JUMPING

To prevent puppies from jumping

1. When your new puppy initially jumps up on you or others, do not react verbally or physically to him. **Ignore** the behavior! Ignore him! If he realizes that he will get no reaction from you, good or bad, there will be no incentive for him to continue to jump!

2. Avoid picking your puppy up or placing him onto your lap because this teaches him that it is okay to come up on top of you.

3. When you or others greet your puppy, bend down to his level.

4. Always use your training **leash** to keep control of your puppy.

If jumping up has been allowed and has become a habit, in addition to the above preventive measures keep your dog attached to you by a six foot training leash and utilize the following techniques.

1. When the dog begins to jump up **immediately** give a quick snap of the leash and in a firm tone say, "**No**" or "**Off.**" (Do not use the word "Down" as this is the command for lying down.) Then, command him to "Sit."

2. Make him "Sit" before he gets a "greeting" from you or others. Eventually, he will make the association between sitting and getting a greeting and this will become a **good** habit.

3. When initially **greeting** the puppy or dog, do it in a **subdued** manner. If you act excited, so will he!

EXCESSIVE BARKING

For a dog, barking is a **normal** means of communication. Dogs bark for a number of reasons.

1. To get **attention** from you, another person or animal.

2. In **response** to a stimulus such as the wind blowing, leaves falling, or squirrels running.

3. As an **alarm** to a perceived threat such as cars passing, a knock on the door, or people walking by.

To prevent excessive barking

1. Do not respond **vocally** to your dog when he looks at you and barks. If you talk to him, he may "answer" you with more barking.

In your experience, if your dog barks as a signal for you to let him out to relieve himself, again, do not start a "conversation" with him. Just take him out!

2. Limit the amount of time your puppy or dog is alone and exposed to outside stimuli without your supervision.

3. Teach your dog the command "**Quiet**" early in his training program.

When he barks longer than what you have decided to be acceptable, give a quick snap of the leash and say, "**Quiet**" in a commanding tone. Give him lots of **praise** when he stops barking.

This lesson, if implemented correctly, **will not** inhibit your dog from barking when it is needed for security purposes.

It will give you the **ability** to **turn** the **alarm** "**off**."

Once you acknowledge, in response to his warning barks that the situation is safe give the command "Quiet" and follow it with lots of praise when he responds.

DIGGING

Digging is a **natural and normal** behavior for dogs.

Dogs dig:

1. to bury food and other "treasures"
2. to find food
3. to expose cool dirt to lie down in on hot days, or make a warm spot to nest in on cold days.
4. out of boredom
5. to expend pent up energy

Because it is a natural instinct, it may not be possible to totally eradicate a dog's tendency to dig.

Utilizing our techniques can enable you to manage and control your dog's need to dig.

To prevent digging

1. Keep your puppy or untrained dog attached to you with his 30- foot cotton training leash when you are outside. Allow him to roam and explore while he is on the leash. If he begins to dig, correct him **immediately** with a quick snap of the leash and a firm "No!" Immediately divert your dog's attention to one of his outside toys.

A correction given **during** the act combined with a subsequent positive substitution is the

most effective way of teaching your dog not to dig.

Exercise **caution** when using the 30-foot leash to avoid entanglements with you and others. For your dog's safety **never** tie him to anything.

2. Provide **proper, interactive play** and **exercise** for your dog or puppy to help him burn off excess energy **before** leaving him in a "safe" outside area. Avoid leaving him outside, unattended for a long period of time.

3. Provide appropriate toys outside for his diversion.

4. Provide a dog house or other type of protection for **shade** from the sun or **shelter** from the elements to keep him warm and dry.

During hot weather, you can use a hard plastic kiddie pool containing a small amount of water so that he can splash, lay down and **cool** off.

5. Avoid gardening if your dog is watching you! Our Welsh corgi thinks she is helping us whenever we do any planting or weeding by digging up plants behind us. Unfortunately, though she is an accomplished "weeder," she can't discriminate between good and bad "weeds!"

If your dog is already in the habit of digging, in addition to the above steps:

1. Try using a **safe** commercial repellent specifically made to keep dogs away from "favorite" areas. Some cooking spices, such as ground ginger or pepper, sprinkled over the area may help.

These "deterrents" need to be used for a period of **at least** 30 days. Wind, rain and snow can dissipate these products and they must be **replaced immediately**. Over time, periodic re-applications may be necessary.

2. Protect flower beds, trees or shrubs by blocking your dog's access to them with fencing.

SUBMISSIVE URINATION

Sometimes puppies will urinate when they become very excited or as an overly submissive response to their owners and other people. This is referred to as "Submissive Urination."

A **prompt** and **correct response** to this behavior when it **first** becomes evident will help you to control and in most cases, alleviate the condition.

1. Rule out any **medical cause** that may be contributing to a lack of bladder control (urinary tract infection or genetic physical anomaly).

2. Do not assume an overly dominant or threatening posture when interacting with your puppy or dog.

3. Ignore your puppy whenever he acts in a submissive manner. Responding to **submissive behavior,** either verbally or physically, can further exacerbate the problem.

4. Don't talk to or **excite** your puppy when you come home or let him out of his crate. Take him outside immediately and give him a chance to relieve himself **before** you give him a greeting.

5. When greeting other people, **do not** let the puppy get **overexcited.**

Teach him to "Sit" and "Stay" next to you for 2-3 minutes. Then release him and **let the puppy approach the person on his own.** Do not talk to him and do not let the other person reach down to pet him, excite him or talk to him. Give the puppy a few minutes more before the "new" person **calmly** acknowledges him.

With our techniques you should see an improvement within a month. Be **patient** and understand that puppies learn and develop in different amounts of time.

As with any behavior modification technique, the **results depend** on **your experience** and ability to **diagnose** the problem and **affect** the treatment.

We **encourage** you to seek professional help whenever you feel the need. "Sooner is better than later!"

SHYNESS

Prior **negative experiences** with people, places, other dogs or animals can cause your dog to be tentative in certain situations.

The **genetic makeup** of a puppy or dog can contribute to the development of shyness.

The **lack** of proper socialization is a common reason for shyness in dogs.

To help prevent shyness

1. Properly socialize your puppy according to the techniques we have outlined in this text. (Chapter 3, Socialization, pp. 42-46.)

2. Obedience train your dog. The more focused he is on you and your **commands** the less concerned he will be with his own anxieties. This will help him to be **calm** and **confident** and to feel **secure** in all situations.

3. When interacting with your puppy or dog, avoid **loud** or **threatening** overtures which can make your dog nervous and shy.

If your dog is already exhibiting shy behavior **immediately** consult your veterinarian or a competent dog trainer experienced with this type of problem.

There is much that **can** be done to **improve** the reactions and state of mind of a shy puppy or dog.

CHAPTER 4

"DOUBLE DOGS"

ADDING A SECOND DOG TO YOUR FAMILY

It is **intelligent** and **kind** to give **serious**
thought to the purchase or adoption of a **new**

puppy or dog. **Many** a dog is given up because of a **hurried** decision or **impulse** purchase by a well-meaning owner.

Exceedingly **more** thought and a **thorough evaluation** of the entire situation is **vital** before deciding to acquire an **additional** puppy or dog.

Consider getting a second dog because **you** and your **family** will enjoy having an additional dog and **not** because you think your dog needs a relationship with another dog!

A dog that is well cared for and receives enough interactive exercise, obedience training and play from his human "family" does not need another dog to be "happy."

Your motivation for getting a second dog should **not** be because you hope or believe that this will solve existing behavior problems in your current dog. Dogs tend to learn from each other and you may end up with two dogs exhibiting the same problem behaviors.

Once you have decided to get a second dog, critical **observation** and **preparation** is necessary for the **successful** introduction of a new puppy or dog into your existing dog's domain.

1. Your **existing dog** should **respond** to your

commands in a fashion that you find totally acceptable. He should **not** display any **inappropriate** behaviors that annoy or concern you. Dogs can copy each other's responses, both good and bad.

Be prepared to go through a comprehensive **training** program with your new dog.

2. Give your **first** dog at least one year to **bond** and **socialize** with your family and other people **before** you acquire a second puppy or dog. Otherwise, the dogs may tend to form a stronger bond with each other than with you and become more "dog" oriented instead of "people" oriented.

3. Confirm through your observations that your current dog enjoys and **accepts** the type of puppy or dog that you are considering. Our definition of **type** includes disposition, breed, size, sex and age.

Dogs of the opposite sex are more likely to be compatible with each other because they occupy different roles within the "pack." Though this arrangement usually works best, dogs of the same sex can and in many cases do get along just fine.

4. Purchase or adopt a new dog only after you have made a choice based on the above criteria. Ask the owner of the dog you are considering if it is possible to bring your current dog to meet the new puppy or dog. (Keep your dog under control on a leash.)

If they get along, great! If not, it may be best to try again with another dog.

5. Initial **control** and **management** of **both** dogs is very important when bringing the new dog home. This is best accomplished by having one dog on a 6-ft. training **leash** attached to you and the second dog also on a 6-ft. training leash attached to another person. For the first "meeting" a **neutral territory** outside of the house may be best to avoid conflicts with possessiveness associated with the first dog's "domain." Slowly allow the dogs to approach each another. Closely observe their response to each other. If it is apparent that their reactions are positive, cautiously allow them to further "investigate" each other.

When inside the house continue to **control** both dogs initially on their leashes. You must be aware of the possibility of potential disputes that can arise over food, toys or even your attention that could escalate into an aggressive confrontation between the two dogs.

Feed them from separate dishes under close supervision to avoid disputes over food as well as the possibility of one dog overeating.

Make sure you spend **time alone** with each dog. Dogs can develop separation anxiety over being away from each other as well as from their owner. (Separation Anxiety pp. 47-50.) Teach them that it is okay to be alone without the constant company of you or the other dog.

You must always be in the position to **control** and **manage** both dogs even if they enjoy each other. There is bound to be a periodic squabble as there is in any family relationship. Don't let their "arguments" escalate. Like people, dogs **need** and respect fair and consistent **leadership**.

CHAPTER 5

HOUSEBREAKING

THE "Pure and Simple" METHOD

The most effective method for the prevention of housebreaking problems is the implementation of a humane and proven training program.

We have previously published a book on this subject titled **HOUSEBREAKING "Pure and Simple"©**. Because of our concern for your success, we have decided to include our method in this text.

In developing this method, we have drawn from our experience in working with thousands of dogs of all sizes, breeds and ages, their owner's needs, the input of practicing veterinarians and scientific data available through veterinary school behavior clinics.

Our program can be initiated when your puppy

is **eight weeks of age** and is also proven **effective** for **older** puppies and dogs of all types and sizes.

Our program will result in a puppy or dog that eliminates quickly on command and controls its body functions for a reasonable amount of time that can exceed eight hours.

Essential Veterinary Care

Veterinary care is necessary to ensure quick and lasting success with any housebreaking program.

The majority of dogs that defecate or urinate in the house do so because they were never properly housebroken. However, there can be a medical reason for a dog to defecate or urinate inappropriately, so it is important to **rule out** any current **medical conditions** that may contribute to problems in housebreaking your dog.

A dog or puppy that is exhibiting more than a normal need to urinate may have cystitis or another urinary tract disease. Intestinal parasites can cause diarrhea, inconsistent stools or a more frequent need to defecate.

As dogs age, senility and incontinence due to decreasing hormonal levels can cause disruptions in housebreaking. Though less common, certain metabolic diseases such as diabetes, can cause dogs or puppies to drink more water and consequently, urinate more.

Proper Diet and Treats

Diet: There is a direct correlation between what "goes in" to what "comes out." Your choice of dog food and treats is very important to your housebreaking success.

Certain foods can have a tendency to result in larger amounts or increased frequency of bowel movements. Individual dogs can vary in the way they metabolize dog food.

Discussing your specific dog's needs with your veterinarian, breeder or pet shop professional is **essential** in making this important decision.

Avoid sudden dietary changes and additions because this can change the consistency of the stool and increase your dog's need to defecate.

As your puppy grows, his intake of food will need to be increased. Do this slowly, in small increments, and you should not experience any adverse effects on housebreaking.

Treats: Feeding too many treats can make it difficult for your dog or puppy to control himself because he will produce more stool.

Here is a good tip. Many dogs interpret getting one little piece of dog food as something "special." Put aside a few pieces of his daily ration of dog food and use them for "treats." He will be getting a "treat" without increasing his daily recommended food intake.

Method

The most important lesson for you to learn is to **keep control** of your puppy or untrained dog **at all times**.

Whenever the dog or puppy is not in his **crate**, he must be on a **six-foot training leash with you holding the other end**.

Yes! All the time, even when he is eating, drinking and playing. By doing this, the dog can never be out of your sight or control. Should the dog start to relieve himself in the house you are in the position to immediately make the proper correction. Quickly snap the leash and in a calm, firm tone of voice say "No!" Then take the dog directly outside to his designated elimination area.

The correction is for the purpose of getting his **attention** and is most effective if given while he is in the process of having the "accident." If the leash is not held in your hand, when your dog has an accident you **cannot** effectively give an immediate correction. You will have to run after the dog in order to correct him. This will teach the dog to **run away** from you. As a result of anticipating the chase and correction, the dog can become **aggressive** or **shy**.

When you cannot be attached to your puppy or untrained dog, he should be in his crate or "safe" outside area.

Many owners are anxious at the thought of leaving a dog in a crate. **Teach** your dog to be comfortable in his crate (Chapter 1, Crate, pp. 5-9.)

Do not talk to your dog after you put him in the crate, while he is in the crate or when you first take him out of the crate. Doing so may get him excited and he may urinate or develop other problems associated with separation anxiety (Chapter 3, Separation Anxiety, p. 48.)

If he should relieve himself in the crate, do not scold him. Stay calm. Take him out of the crate, clean the mess and use an odor neutralizer to get rid of any trace odor in the crate. If necessary, clean the dog.

Teaching a puppy or dog where and when to

relieve himself is done in the following way.

1. Dress appropriately so that you can comfortably stay outside with your dog. He must learn to eliminate during bad as well as good weather.

2. Use the same door to go outside when taking the puppy out to urinate and defecate. This will help him identify going out for the specific purpose of voiding.

3. Choose a specific area outside that will be used specifically for elimination only. Go directly to this area with the dog on his leash and **stand in one place.** Do not move! By allowing your puppy or dog to investigate or sniff around a larger area, he will become distracted by different sights and scents and not fully concentrate on voiding.

Initially leave a small amount of feces down to help the puppy to identify "his spot." Keep the remaining area clean. Dogs do not relish stepping in feces any more than you do. This will also help in controlling the spread of intestinal parasites.

4. Repeat a phrase in a quiet, monotone voice such as "Do your business . . . Do your business." Use this one or make up your own but always use the same phrase. You want the puppy to

associate your particular **phrase** with the actual **process** of elimination. Later on, this will be helpful in getting him to **eliminate quickly** on command whenever he hears the phrase.

5. Continue repeating the phrase until he starts to void. **Be silent** while he is urinating or defecating. Wait until he is completely finished and then **vocally praise, praise, praise!** Dogs respond very quickly to your tone of voice, so if you start to praise him during the act he may become distracted and stop.

Allow a **ten minute period** for your dog to relieve himself. Training him to go quickly when first taken outside will give you control of your valuable time. By taking long walks or playing with the puppy **before** he voids, you are forming a habit that you may not always be able to keep because of weather conditions, illness or time restrictions.

If he has **not relieved** himself within the ten minute time frame, bring him directly back into the house. Don't stay out any longer. Keep him inside until the next scheduled elimination "walk." (Refer to Housebreaking Schedule, p. 87.) **Watch** him closely for any sign that he may need to relieve himself such as circling, smelling the floor, staring at you or pulling toward the door. If so indicated, bring him back outside to his elimination area and repeat the entire process.

Avoid taking him out more frequently than your schedule indicates for an elimination walk if he is not signaling a need to do so. Otherwise, he may never learn to control himself for any long period of time.

For the first two weeks that you begin the program, you should give the puppy an extra two minutes after he has relieved himself to make sure that he has completely finished the process. Many owners rush inside too quickly, only to have the puppy finish inside what he started to do outside.

Once the puppy or dog has relieved himself in the designated area, then it is time for **exercise** and **play**.

Housebreaking Schedule

Consistency and continuity are essential to successfully housebreak your puppy or untrained dog.

The schedule we have outlined has accommodated thousands of owners and their dogs. Revise it to coincide with your lifestyle, adjusting the times, within reason, to suit your own needs.

If you are not available to walk your dog as often as indicated by our schedule, do not fret. Puppies will eventually develop enough physical control to become housebroken. However, if you are away from the house for a long period of time (exceeding 8 hours) consider hiring a responsible dog walker for at least one midday elimination walk and some playtime or arrange for "puppy day care" at a boarding kennel or your veterinarian's office.

Scheduling the intake of food and water makes it easier for a puppy to control himself. It is more humane than allowing him unlimited access to food and water with no chance to urinate or defecate outside. This approach is safe and effective for normal puppies and dogs. If you have any doubts or concerns about managing food and water intake please consult your veterinarian.

When feeding your puppy, keep the food and water down on the floor in front of him for a period of fifteen minutes. This will allow the dog plenty of opportunity to eat and drink. Take up whatever he does not finish until the next scheduled time.

Immediately after eating and drinking, puppies and dogs should be taken out to eliminate regardless of when they last urinated or defecated. The reason for this is that dogs, like people, after eating or drinking can experience a gastrointestinal reflex with a resultant need to void.

Though not on the schedule provided, there are a few other times that you may need to bring your puppy or dog out for an elimination walk:

For puppies less than four months of age:
1. After a nap
2. After a treat
3. Before and after indoor playtime as activity may stimulate the need to void.

For dogs of any age:
Any time indicated by the dog's behavior or signals, such as circling, pulling toward the door, sniffing the floor.

Example Schedule

Time	Activity
7am	elimination walk
	play, exercise
8am	food, water, elimination walk
	play, exercise
11am	water, elimination walk
	play, exercise
2pm	water, elimination walk
	play, exercise
5pm	food, water, elimination walk,
	play, exercise
8pm	water, elimination walk
	play, exercise
11pm	elimination walk

As you see, we have suggested **exercise** and **play** frequently in this schedule. This will result in a dog that is **calmer** in the house and a **happier** you!

HOUSEBREAKING "MISTAKES"

RUB HIS NOSE IN IT

Based on many years of experience in housebreaking dogs, we find that this way of trying to communicate your displeasure over the dog's mistake is ineffective and may very well cause the development of **aggression and/or shyness** toward you. We strongly advise against this.

CORRECTIONS AFTER THE FACT

There are some people who conclude that dogs remember old misdeeds and therefore, can be scolded after the fact. This method of correction is rarely effective in teaching the dog not to eliminate in the house.

So many times owners will say that the dog looks or acts guilty when they return home to find an "accident" in the house. They interpret this to mean that the dog knows he did wrong. The owner's negative body language, facial expressions and tone of voice are the actual cause of the dog's anxiety. The dog is responding simply to what the owner is doing and not to what he has done. Dogs can shy away from you or "act" guilty or fearful after they have relieved themselves in the house, anticipating your anger and punishment.

SMALL BREEDS

There exists a myth that small dogs can't be housebroken. The fact is that they possess as much intelligence and physical ability to become housebroken as any large dog. Owners of small dogs may tend to accept or overlook small accidents for a longer period of time, making it more difficult to effect successful housebreaking.

TWO WEEKS AND TRAINED

There are people who believe that a dog is housebroken if he has been "clean" in the house for a period of a few weeks. For the most part, what actually happens is that the dog has been good for a couple of weeks and based on this, the owners have given him freedom in the house. The dog begins to have accidents since he was actually not completely housebroken in the first place. The owners control the dog for another few weeks and he's good again so he's given his freedom once more. The cycle repeats itself over and over, creating a dog that will never be totally housebroken.

Important to Remember

We would like to tell you that your puppy or dog will be housebroken within a certain period of time. However, the truth is that like children being "Potty trained" puppies are individuals and will become housebroken within varying lengths of time.

Adhere to the housebreaking principles until your puppy or dog has had absolutely **no "accidents"** for a period of **at least twelve consecutive weeks.**

Our experience indicates that most dogs that are not housebroken are also not very well behaved. Those that are obedient and well behaved tend to be housebroken.

As a result of controlling your puppy for housebreaking purposes, you will be in the best position to teach and enforce obedience commands.

CHAPTER 6

MISCONCEPTIONS

Early Training

It has always been our recommendation that puppies can and should begin training at **eight weeks of age.** Our experience has proven this recommendation true. Scientific studies have confirmed that puppies actually have mature brain wave patterns by five weeks of age and thus are fully capable of learning!

It is **much easier** to form good habits in a **young, impressionable** and **physically pliable** puppy than to try and correct established bad habits in a physically stronger, older dog.

Two Weeks And Trained

Many owners believe that if their dog has been well behaved for a few weeks time that he is trained. This is **false!**

It takes a **minimum** of **six months to one year** for a puppy or untrained dog to **learn** not only commands and appropriate **behaviors,** but to have experienced enough **positive reinforcements** over a period of time and in numerous and various circumstances to proclaim him **"trained."**

On/Off Leash Training

Having your dog obey commands on the leash, with and without distractions, is a major accomplishment.

However, just because he listens perfectly **"on leash"** (basic training) **does not** mean he will automatically listen when commands are given **"off leash"** (advanced training.)

Off leash training is a totally **separate process** that requires additional time and effort. Be **prudent** where and when you let your dog off the leash! Even the best trained dog can become confused or startled in new situations and environments, **run off, get lost, injured** or **killed.**

Older Dogs Cannot Learn New Tricks

Of course **they can!** Many times it is easier for them to change than for their owners! The reason for this is that we **can** control the dog's behavior, environment, and training conditions. The challenge comes in controlling and changing **our own habits, reactions** and **attitudes** toward our pets.

I have personally trained many older dogs, 6, 7, 8, 9, 10 years of age and even a **14-year-old** deaf, crossbred dog that was blind in one eye! He loved every minute of the training and **did great**!

The Quick Fix

In our experience there is **no "quick-trick fix"** training method that is safe, humane, effective and suitable for all dogs and puppies.

So called "quick-fixes" will in many cases be totally ignored by the dog or can create **unwanted** side effects such as **aggression** or **shyness**. Quick fixes usually do not offer **lasting** results and **cannot** be **safely** implemented by **all** members of the family.

Food Rewards

Many dogs will become **distracted** by food rewards and may **not perform** correctly unless the food is available.

The use of "**people food**" can create undesirable behaviors such as begging or "stealing" food.

Food rewards can have a place in training, teaching tricks, and behavior modification programs **but** the use of food should be initiated with the help of a professional trainer or behaviorist to avoid the development of problems.

Anyone Can Train Their Dog On Their Own

The truth is **most** people **cannot** successfully train their dog to their complete satisfaction without some form of professional instruction. Unless you are very experienced in the art of training dogs of various temperaments, sizes, ages and breeds, you may become frustrated, short-tempered and give up or force an issue and create a bad situation.

Be smart! Let a professional help you from the beginning with **at least** one training session. This will give you the opportunity to actually **experience** the **correct** way to **physically implement** training techniques and hear the **correct tone** of voice that is necessary for commanding, correcting and praising your dog. It will **hasten** and facilitate the training process and the **result** will be more to your original expectations.

Great Expectations

Unfortunately, many owners expect their dogs to always behave and react in an excellent fashion. This is not realistic. As with people,

"Nobody's perfect!"

We all love our dogs. And, because we do, we should realize that they will not always act or react perfectly in all situations, at all times. **Forgive them** their little imperfections. **Be tolerant** and **patient. Help them** to maintain their obedience skills and control their exuberance when and where it is necessary.

Stupid, Spiteful, Stubborn

We have had the opportunity to face the most challenging of conflicts between dogs and their owners, and can attest to the fact that dogs are **not stupid**.

We have **never** met a dog that could not learn the basic, on leash obedience commands to sit, stand, down, stay, heel and come. The owner and sometimes even the professional may not have the know-how, experience, or the degree of patience necessary for the more **challenging** of dogs and their problems.

Because of their genetic makeup, certain breeds and individual dogs may be more willing to accept direction than others. Like people, dogs learn at different paces. Puppies have shorter attention spans and older dogs can have habits to be changed and behavior issues to be resolved.

The human term "**spite**," by definition, means to "treat maliciously." Isn't it wonderful that our canine companions **are not** capable of this emotion?

Dogs **do not** act out of spite. The destructive chewing, excessive barking or inappropriate elimination that occurs when you are home or when the dog is home alone is more likely a manifestation of **improper training, separation anxiety** or an inadequate amount of **interactive play, exercise** and **obedience** work.

Dogs are not **stubborn**. "Stubborn" is a negative term that indicates a conscious effort to be difficult.

When dogs don't listen it's because:

a) they were **never properly taught** by their owner to consistently obey every time, all the time, in every situation. Just because a dog responds to a command sometimes, it does not mean that he knows to obey all the time.

b) they are completely preoccupied with something else (a new smell, taste, person, animal, play or some other distraction.)

"Show Him Who's The Boss!"

Yes, it is essential that you become your dog's leader but physical intimidation (shaking by the scruff, hitting, yelling at, throwing things) is **not necessary** or recommended. This can result in **shyness** and **aggression.**

Dogs tend to follow consistent leadership. It is okay to be firm with your dog. Yes, be in charge of your dog. Yes, be his leader. **But** remember to do so in a **fair, kind and understanding** way!

When your dog complies, always shower him with lots of **praise, praise, praise.**

Dogs Can Eat Anything They Want

No! Control what your dog or puppy ingests. Though he may want to chew and eat rocks, sticks, bones, and other foreign objects, allowing this can result in diarrhea, vomiting, poisoning, intestinal obstruction or other digestive tract disorders. These are **serious** and sometimes **fatal** medical problems.

Feeding your dog human food can cause medical problems as well.

Your Dog Will Let You Know When He's Sick

Your dog **may not** appear obviously ill to you until he is **very** sick. Watch for **subtle** changes in his weight, appetite or attitude.

Symptoms such as intermittent vomiting, diarrhea or increased thirst may appear mild and of no real concern at first, but can be **early** manifestations of a more serious medical condition.

CHAPTER 7

POINTS TO REMEMBER

Though you may **intellectually** comprehend the methods and philosophy that we have presented the actual **physical application** of **any** training and behavior modification technique can prove to be more of a challenge.

The **results** you achieve are not solely dependent on how much you love your dog, but rather on a **combination** of **factors**.

The **understanding** of your dog's individual temperament, behavior and reactions, your **knowledge** of his breed's characteristics and your **experience** and **ability** to implement training techniques will all have an effect on your **success**.

Be **kind**, **tolerant** and **patient** with your dog. In most cases, his **response** is the **direct result** of **your** ability as a dog trainer.

Be **patient** with yourself because in many

cases you are **learning** as well as **teaching**.

Don't be afraid to ask for help and don't wait until the situation gets out of hand.

We **strongly encourage** you to have **at least** one session with a qualified, professional dog trainer to **observe** the actual **physical** application of training and behavior techniques as they apply to you and your dog.

This will **maximize** your efforts and **enhance** your results.

Be realistic in your expectations. Your dog may not always be perfect, but you should **always** be able to **control him** and have him act in a **civil** and **socially acceptable** manner.

Successful businesses, families, and individuals practice good management and exercise good control.

Well-behaved dogs are well managed and controllable.

Keep your pup **safe and under control** on the **leash** attached to you, **inside** as well as **outside**, for the **first year** of his life.

Do this for at least **six months** with an

older, untrained dog.

When you cannot be with him, he should be kept in a **"safe"** and **secure** place such as his crate or secured area of the yard.

The last two months of this type of control should be **free** of any undesirable behaviors and should find your dog responding to obedience commands to your satisfaction.

Keep up with required examinations and medical treatments as recommended by your **veterinarian**.

As a **medically aware** owner you will be in the best position to react **quickly** and **positively** to any deviation in your dog's physical well-being and also know how these changes may be affecting his **training** and **behavior.**

We must emphasize the **necessity** for you to **interact** with your dog in play and exercise.

Practice and **utilize** your dog's **training** as you would any of your own skills for continued effectiveness.

Being successful and doing anything

correctly involves work and commitment. Sometimes, it also involves doing things we don't want to do, when we don't feel like doing them.

The **reward** for your efforts will be a dog that is **healthy, confident, calm** and **well behaved** . . . inspiring a **long-lasting** and **satisfying** relationship.

INDEX